THE ULTIMATE
Red Panda
BOOK

BELLANOVA

MELBOURNE · SOFIA · BERLIN

ISBN: 978-619-7695-43-4
Imprint: Bellanova Books

CONTENTS

MEET THE RED PANDAS!

Welcome, dear readers, to the wonderful world of red pandas! These enchanting creatures have captured the hearts of people around the world with their unique appearance, playful nature, and captivating charm.

In this book, we'll take you on an exciting journey to discover everything there is to know about red pandas. From their habitats and physical characteristics to their behavior, diet, and the importance of conservation, we'll explore every aspect of their lives to help you gain a deep understanding and appreciation for these amazing animals.

Discovering Red Panda Mysteries

Throughout our adventure, we'll unravel some of the fascinating mysteries that surround red pandas. Did you know that red pandas are not closely related to their larger namesake, the giant panda? Instead, they belong to their own unique family, Ailuridae. We'll dive into their family tree and uncover the secrets of their evolutionary history.

Exploring Their World

We'll also take you on a virtual trip to the captivating environments where red pandas live. From the lush, misty forests of the Himalayas to the hidden corners of southwestern China, we'll explore the diverse habitats that these creatures call home. Along the way, we'll learn about the amazing adaptations that help them thrive in their unique ecosystems.

Delving into Their Daily Lives

Get ready to uncover the secrets of red panda behavior, social life, and family dynamics. We'll reveal how they communicate, forage for food, and interact with one another in their complex and fascinating world.

Becoming Conservation Champions

Red pandas face numerous challenges in the wild, from habitat loss to poaching. In our journey, we'll learn about the efforts being made to protect these adorable animals and what you can do to help ensure their survival for generations to come.

Celebrate Their Cultural Significance

Finally, we'll delve into the rich history of red pandas in culture and folklore, exploring the stories, beliefs, and traditions that have shaped human perceptions of these captivating creatures.

As we embark on this adventure together, we hope to spark a passion for red pandas in readers young and old, inspiring a love for these incredible animals and a commitment to their conservation. So, let's get started and enter the world of red pandas!

HIGH ALTITUDE HOMES

Red Panda Habitats

Red pandas inhabit the temperate forests of the Eastern Himalayas and Southwestern China, which stretch across Nepal, Bhutan, India, Myanmar, and Tibet. These regions are characterized by steep slopes and high elevations, typically ranging from 4,900 to 13,000 feet (1,500 to 4,000 meters) above sea level. Red pandas thrive in these high-altitude environments, where dense bamboo forests provide them with shelter, food, and protection from predators.

A Haven of Bamboo: The Red Panda's Pantry

Bamboo is the primary source of energy for red pandas, making up around 95% of their diet. Consequently, their habitats must have plenty of bamboo for them to survive. Bamboo forests in these regions are lush and thick, with a diverse variety of bamboo species, such as  Himalayacalamus, Yushania, and Arundinaria. These bamboo-rich habitats not only supply red pandas with food but also offer them excellent hiding spots and safe havens to build their nests.

Cozy Nests: A Red Panda's Hideaway

Within their bamboo habitats, red pandas construct nests to rest, sleep, and rear their young. These nests are usually built in the hollows of trees or in the forks of branches, high above the ground to keep them safe from ground-dwelling predators.

Red pandas line their nests with leaves, moss, and other soft materials to create a warm and comfortable space for themselves and their cubs.

Did you know...?

Red pandas not only build their cozy nests high up in trees to avoid predators but also cleverly choose locations close to their favorite food source, bamboo. This allows them to have easy access to their primary diet without having to venture too far from their safe and snug hideaway!

Sharing Space: Neighbors in the Forest

Red pandas are not the only inhabitants of these high-altitude forests. They share their habitat with a diverse range of wildlife, including other endangered species like the snow leopard, clouded leopard, and Himalayan black bear.

These animals often coexist in the same ecosystems, relying on the forest's resources for food and shelter.

By protecting red panda habitats, conservation efforts can also benefit the many other species that call these forests home.

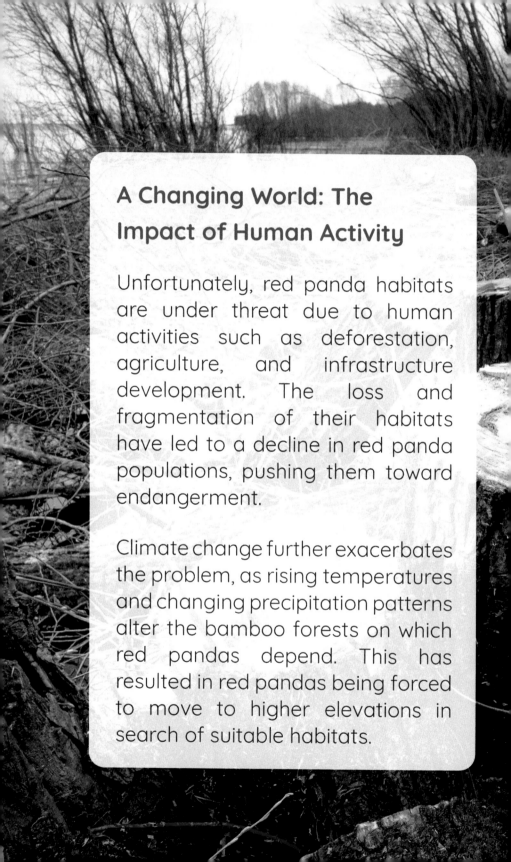

A Changing World: The Impact of Human Activity

Unfortunately, red panda habitats are under threat due to human activities such as deforestation, agriculture, and infrastructure development. The loss and fragmentation of their habitats have led to a decline in red panda populations, pushing them toward endangerment.

Climate change further exacerbates the problem, as rising temperatures and changing precipitation patterns alter the bamboo forests on which red pandas depend. This has resulted in red pandas being forced to move to higher elevations in search of suitable habitats.

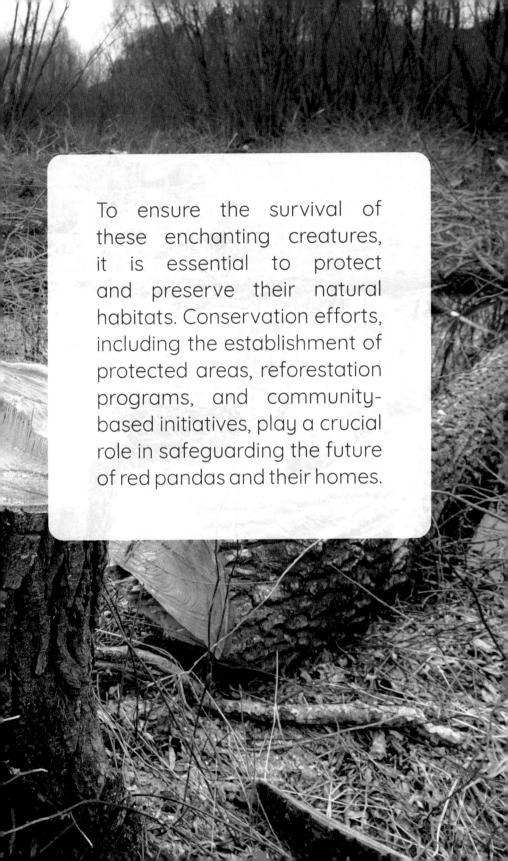

To ensure the survival of these enchanting creatures, it is essential to protect and preserve their natural habitats. Conservation efforts, including the establishment of protected areas, reforestation programs, and community-based initiatives, play a crucial role in safeguarding the future of red pandas and their homes.

MEET THE COUSINS

Red Panda Subspecies

Did you know that there are two subspecies of red pandas? That's right! These adorable creatures share many similarities but also have some distinct differences. In this chapter, we'll introduce you to the two subspecies of red pandas: **Ailurus fulgens fulgens** and **Ailurus fulgens styani**. We'll explore their unique characteristics, habits, and habitats, and learn what makes each one special.

WHICH SUBSPECIES AM I?

Answer: Himalayan red panda.

The Himalayan red panda's whiter coat helps it blend into its mountain habitat, providing better camouflage against potential predators.

HIMALAYAN RED PANDA

Scientific name: *Ailurus fulgens fulgens*

Habitat and Range

The Himalayan red panda can be found in the lush, misty forests of the eastern Himalayas. They inhabit countries such as Nepal, Bhutan, and northeastern India, where they roam the temperate forests at elevations between 4,900 and 13,000 feet (1,500 and 4,000 meters).

Physical Features

The Himalayan red panda has a slightly lighter coat color compared to its cousin, the Chinese red panda. Their fur is more muted and their facial markings are less distinct. However, they still have the same adorable features, like the bushy tail and expressive eyes that red pandas are famous for.

19

CHINESE RED PANDA

Scientific name: *Ailurus fulgens styani*

Habitat and Range

The second subspecies, the Chinese red panda, calls southwestern China and northern Myanmar home. These pandas prefer similar habitats to their Eastern Himalayan relatives, living in temperate forests with dense bamboo undergrowth.

Physical Features

The Chinese red panda sports a more vibrant reddish coat, giving it a slightly bolder appearance. Their facial markings are more pronounced, with darker, more distinct "tear tracks" under their eyes. These features make the Chinese red panda easy to distinguish from its Eastern Himalayan counterpart.

The Chinese red panda has a longer tail than the Himalayan red panda, which helps it to balance and maneuver more efficiently through the dense forests of southwestern China, where it lives.

Similarities and Shared Challenges

Despite the differences in their physical appearance and their geographical range, both subspecies of red pandas share many similarities. They have the same diet, primarily consisting of bamboo, and exhibit similar behaviors and social structures.

Both subspecies face the same threats in the wild, including habitat loss, poaching, and climate change.

FURRY *fashionistas*

Physical Characteristics

Red pandas are truly the fashion icons of the animal kingdom! Their beautiful, thick fur comes in a fabulous mix of colors, ranging from rusty red to deep brown, with touches of black and white to complete the look.

This stylish coat doesn't just make them look great; it also helps them stay warm in their chilly mountain homes and blend into their surroundings. Their fur even covers the soles of their feet, making them extra cozy and providing traction as they navigate slippery branches.

Ring-a-Ding-Ding: That Marvelous Tail

Have you ever seen a tail as cool as the red panda's? Their bushy, ringed tails are not only eye-catching but also serve a practical purpose. The alternating light and dark rings on their tails work as fantastic camouflage among the dappled sunlight of the forest. These magnificent tails also help red pandas balance while they're climbing trees and leaping from branch to branch.

Did you know...?

Red pandas' large, round eyes are suited for low-light conditions, making it easier for them to spot food and keep an eye out for danger during their foraging adventures.

Paws-itively Amazing: Red Panda Paws

Red pandas have some pretty incredible paws, perfectly designed for their tree-hopping lifestyle. Their sharp, semi-retractable claws help them grip onto branches and climb with ease. The coolest feature, though, is their "false thumb." Red pandas have a specialized, extended wrist bone that works like an extra digit, allowing them to hold onto bamboo stalks as they munch away. With these amazing paws, red pandas are true acrobats of the forest!

Expressive Faces: The Red Panda's Signature Look

One look at a red panda's face, and it's hard not to fall in love! Their expressive faces feature white markings around the eyes and mouth, along with reddish-brown fur on their cheeks and forehead.

Size Matters: Small but Mighty

Red pandas may look like a mix between a raccoon, a fox, and a panda, but they're actually quite small. On average, they're about 20 to 26 inches (50 to 66 cm) long, not including their tails, which can be an additional 12 to 20 inches (30 to 50 cm) in length.

Red pandas typically weigh between 7 and 14 pounds (3 to 6 kg), making them much smaller than their distant relative, the giant panda. Despite their small size, red pandas are strong climbers and expert navigators of their high-altitude homes.

A BAMBOO BUFFET
DIET &
FORAGING

When it comes to food, red pandas are true bamboo connoisseurs! Bamboo makes up a whopping 95% of their diet, and they love nothing more than munching on tender, juicy leaves. With their keen sense of smell, red pandas can easily sniff out the freshest, most delicious bamboo in the forest.

They use their amazing "false thumb" to grip onto bamboo stalks and strip off the leaves with their sharp teeth.

Branching Out: A Diverse Diet

Although bamboo is their main food source, red pandas aren't picky eaters. They like to branch out and try new things from time to time. When the opportunity arises, red pandas will feast on fruits, berries, and even tasty flowers!

They'll also snack on insects, bird eggs, and small animals, adding some protein to their otherwise plant-based diet. This diverse menu keeps red pandas happy, healthy, and full of energy for their tree-climbing escapades.

Did you know...?

These little guys can eat up to one-third of their body weight in bamboo leaves each day!

Climbing for Calories: Foraging Adventures

Foraging for food is no walk in the park for red pandas. They have to work hard to find enough food to fuel their active lifestyles. Red pandas spend most of their waking hours searching for food in the trees and on the ground, climbing up and down the forest's many layers. They use their agile bodies and sharp claws to navigate the forest with ease, leaping from branch to branch in search of their next meal.

Feeding Frenzy: Eating Around the Clock

Red pandas are crepuscular eaters, which means they're most active during the early morning and late afternoon when it comes to finding food. This is when the forest is at its quietest, giving them the perfect opportunity to munch away without worrying about predators. However, red pandas are known to snack throughout the day and night as well, making sure they get all the nutrients they need to stay healthy and strong.

Adapting to the Seasons: Changing Food Sources

As the seasons change, so does the red panda's diet. In warmer months, fresh bamboo leaves are abundant, making it easy for red pandas to find their favorite food. But when winter comes, and the bamboo leaves become scarce, red pandas have to adapt. They'll switch from eating leaves to munching on bamboo shoots and even the bark of the plants.

This adaptability helps red pandas survive and thrive, no matter the season.

LONE RANGERS

Behaviour & Social Life

You might think that red pandas would love hanging out together, but they're actually quite the introverts! These furry creatures prefer to spend most of their time alone, only coming together for short periods during the mating season.

They live a peaceful life, roaming their territories and seeking out the best spots for food, shelter, and rest.

THE LANGUAGE OF RED PANDAS

Even though they enjoy their alone time, red pandas still need to communicate with one another. They have a wide range of vocalizations, from squeals and twitters to huffs and grunts, which help them express their feelings and intentions. They also use body language and facial expressions to communicate with their fellow red pandas. When they're feeling playful, they might engage in a friendly game of "tag" among the trees or groom each other as a sign of affection.

SCENT-SATIONAL MARKINGS: CLAIMING THEIR TERRITORY

Red pandas have a unique way of letting others know where they've been: scent markings! They have scent glands located at the base of their tails, which produce a smelly liquid that they use to mark their territory. By rubbing their tails on trees, rocks, and other surfaces, red pandas can leave a scent trail for others to follow. This helps them track their territories and avoid accidentally wandering into a neighbor's space.

TREE-DWELLERS: MASTERS OF THE TREETOPS

One of the most striking aspects of red panda behavior is their incredible tree-climbing skills. They're expert acrobats, using their sharp claws and strong limbs to move gracefully through the forest

canopy. They can even climb down trees headfirst, thanks to their flexible ankles! Red pandas feel right at home in the trees, where they can rest, eat, and escape from predators.

POWER NAPPERS: RESTING UP FOR ADVENTURE

Red pandas know the importance of a good nap! These cuddly creatures spend a large portion of their day resting and conserving energy for their next foraging session. They can often be found curled up in a cozy tree hollow or draped over a branch, with their fluffy tails wrapped around them for warmth. When they're not snoozing, red pandas are on the move, exploring their territory and searching for food.

REPRODUCTION & LIFE CYCLE

When it comes to romance, red pandas have a specific window of opportunity. Their mating season typically occurs between January and March, when male and female red pandas come together to find a suitable partner.

During this time, males will use their keen sense of smell to track down females, who will leave scent markings to

signal their readiness to mate. Once they find a partner, red pandas will engage in playful behaviors, such as chasing and grooming each other, to strengthen their bond.

Expecting Moms: The Red Panda Pregnancy

After a successful courtship and mating, female red pandas will embark on a new journey: motherhood. The **gestation period** (how long they are pregnant) for red pandas ranges from 90 to 150 days, with variations due to a phenomenon called **"delayed implantation."** This means that the fertilized egg doesn't immediately implant in the mother's uterus, allowing her to time the birth of her cubs according to favorable environmental conditions.

Cute Cubs: The Arrival of Baby Red Pandas

When the time is right, female red pandas will give birth to one to four cubs, usually in a cozy, leaf-lined nest within a tree hollow. At birth, red panda cubs are tiny, weighing only about 4 ounces (110 grams), and covered in soft, light gray fur. They're born blind and helpless, relying entirely on their mother's care and protection for the first few weeks of their lives.

Growing Up: The Red Panda Development Journey

As the weeks go by, red panda cubs undergo some amazing changes. Their eyes open at around 18 days old, and their fur gradually transforms into the beautiful red, black, and white coat we all know and love. By the time they reach three months old, they'll have gained the strength and coordination needed to climb trees and explore their surroundings. Cubs will start learning to forage for food under their mother's watchful eye, gradually transitioning from drinking her milk to eating bamboo and other foods.

Spreading Their Wings: Red Panda Independence

By the time they reach six to eight months old, red panda cubs will have developed the skills and confidence needed to venture out on their own. They'll gradually spend more time away from their mother, eventually establishing their own territories and beginning their solitary adult lives at around one year old. Red pandas usually reach sexual maturity between 18 and 24 months old, at which point they'll be ready to start their own families and continue the cycle of life.

CONSERVATION & THREATS

The struggles of red pandas

Although red pandas are beloved by people around the world, these beautiful animals face some serious challenges in their natural habitats. Human activities, such as deforestation, poaching, and climate change, are putting tremendous pressure on red panda populations, making their future uncertain.

VANISHING HOMES: THE IMPACT OF DEFORESTATION

One of the most significant threats to red pandas is the loss of their forest homes. As humans cut down trees for agriculture, logging, and infrastructure development, red pandas are left with fewer places to live, find food, and raise their young. Fragmented forests can also make it difficult for red pandas to find mates, leading to a decline in their populations.

THE CRUEL TRADE: POACHING AND THE ILLEGAL WILDLIFE MARKET

Despite being protected by law in most countries, red pandas still fall victim to poaching for their beautiful fur and other body parts,

which are often sold on the black market. This cruel and illegal trade not only takes the lives of innocent red pandas but also further threatens the survival of their already vulnerable populations.

A CHANGING CLIMATE: THE EFFECTS OF GLOBAL WARMING

Climate change is another major concern for red pandas. As temperatures rise and weather patterns shift, the bamboo plants that red pandas rely on for food may struggle to grow, resulting in a shortage of their primary food source.

HOPE FOR THE FUTURE

Despite the challenges red pandas face, there's still hope for their survival, thanks to the hard work of dedicated conservationists and organizations. Efforts to protect red pandas and their habitats include reforestation projects, anti-poaching patrols, and community-based conservation initiatives that involve local people in the protection of these amazing animals.

Just a few of the organizations that work hard to protect red pandas and other wildlife. Check out their websites and see how you can get involved!

BECOME A RED PANDA HERO

Everyone can play a role in ensuring a brighter future for red pandas.

Here are some ways you can contribute to their conservation and become a true Red Panda Hero:

Support Conservation Organizations

Help red pandas by supporting organizations that protect them. Donate, adopt a red panda, or purchase merchandise to fund their efforts.

Idea: Ask for donations to a red panda charity instead of gifts for your next birthday or holiday celebration.

Educate Others

Share your love for red pandas and educate friends, family, and classmates about these amazing animals and their challenges.

Idea: Create a presentation or poster about red pandas for your class or community group, or organize a red panda-themed event or fundraiser at your school.

Make Environmentally Friendly Choices

Protect the environment and red panda habitats by recycling, conserving water, and using energy-efficient appliances.

Idea: Start a recycling program at your school or neighborhood or create a fun energy or water-saving challenge in your household.

Support Sustainable Products

Purchase products made from sustainable materials and support eco-friendly companies.

Idea: Organize a "Green Shopping Challenge" with your friends or family to find and purchase eco-friendly products.

Every little bit helps! By getting involved in conservation efforts, spreading awareness, and making eco-friendly choices, you'll play a vital role in ensuring the survival of red pandas.

Together, we can make a brighter future for them!

A DIFFERENT WORLD

Red Pandas in Captivity

While we've explored the lives of red pandas in the wild, many of them also live in zoos and wildlife centers around the world. In this chapter, we'll delve into the world of red pandas in captivity, learning about their care, the role of zoos in conservation efforts, and the challenges they face in adapting to life away from their natural habitats.

CREATING SUITABLE ENVIRONMENTS

Red pandas have unique needs that must be met to ensure their well-being in captivity. Zoos and wildlife centers strive to replicate their natural habitats as closely as possible, providing them with ample space, climbing structures, and vegetation that mimics their forest homes. These enclosures offer the red pandas opportunities to climb, explore, and forage, just like they would in the wild.

FEEDING TIME

Red pandas are known for their specialized diet, primarily consisting of bamboo. In captivity, their caretakers must provide them with a balanced and nutritious diet that meets their specific dietary needs. Bamboo is often supplemented with fruits, vegetables, and specially formulated biscuits to ensure they receive all the necessary nutrients to stay healthy.

CAPTIVE BREEDING PROGRAMS

One of the significant roles that zoos and wildlife centers play in red panda conservation is through captive breeding programs. By carefully managing and coordinating breeding efforts, these institutions can help maintain a healthy and genetically diverse captive population. In some cases, captive-bred red pandas may be reintroduced into the wild to bolster struggling populations, providing a much-needed boost to their numbers.

ENRICHMENT AND WELL-BEING

Captive red pandas require mental and physical stimulation to stay happy and healthy. Zoos and wildlife centers provide enrichment activities to encourage their natural behaviors, such as foraging, problem-solving, and playing.

These activities may include puzzle feeders, hidden treats, and new climbing structures, helping to keep their minds active and engaged.

CHALLENGES OF CAPTIVITY

While zoos and wildlife centers strive to provide the best possible care for red pandas, life in captivity still presents some challenges. Red pandas may be more susceptible to stress and disease in captivity, making it crucial for their caretakers to monitor their health closely and provide appropriate veterinary care. Additionally, educating the public about red pandas and their conservation needs is essential in inspiring action and support for them.

RED PANDAS IN CULTURE

Red pandas have a rich history in the cultures and folklore of the regions where they are found, particularly in the Himalayas and the surrounding areas. These enchanting creatures have captured the imaginations of people for centuries, with their unique appearance and behaviors inspiring countless stories, beliefs, and traditions.

Red Pandas in Nepali Folklore

In Nepal, red pandas are called "Ningaule," meaning "fire cat" or "fire fox." Folklore says their fur has magical powers to protect from evil spirits and bad luck. As guardians of the forests, they protect trees and animals. These beliefs encourage the protection of red pandas and their habitats.

Red Pandas in Bhutanese Culture

In Bhutanese culture, red pandas are linked to shapeshifting mystics called "yogi" or "yogini." They were believed to transform into animals, including red pandas, for undetected forest travel. This connection adds to the perception of red pandas as elusive, mysterious, and magical creatures.

The Red Panda Dance: A Traditional Celebration in Sikkim

In the Indian state of Sikkim, the red panda is a symbol of the region's rich biodiversity and cultural heritage. The annual Red Panda Winter Carnival celebrates the cultural significance of these animals through traditional dance performances, known as the "Red Panda Dance." During this dance, performers wear elaborate red panda costumes and masks while performing acrobatic and playful movements that mimic the red panda's behavior.

Red Pandas as National Symbols

Red pandas have also been adopted as symbols of national pride and conservation awareness in several countries where they are found. In Nepal, the red panda is featured on postage stamps, while in India, it serves as the state animal of Sikkim. These national symbols help to raise awareness about the importance of red panda conservation and the need to protect their habitats for future generations to enjoy.

RED PANDA
FUN FACTS

You've already learned so much about red pandas, but there's still more to discover! Prepare to dive into a treasure trove of fascinating and delightful fun facts about red pandas.

Afterwards, test yourself in the quiz!

Red pandas are not closely related to giant pandas. Despite their shared name, red pandas are more closely related to raccoons, skunks, and weasels.

❧ ❧ ❧

They are the only living member of their taxonomic family, Ailuridae.

❧ ❧ ❧

They have retractable claws, just like a cat.

❧ ❧ ❧

Red pandas are crepuscular, meaning they are most active at dawn and dusk.

They have a unique vocalization called a "twitter," which they use to communicate.

❧ ❧ ❧

Red pandas can taste artificial sweeteners, a rare ability among mammals.

❧ ❧ ❧

They have a specialized digestive system designed to process bamboo, despite being part of the carnivore family.

❧ ❧ ❧

Despite their specialized digestive system to break down bamboo, only about 24% of the bamboo they eat gets digested.

Red pandas can eat up to 200,000 bamboo leaves in a single day.

❧ ❧ ❧

Their red fur helps them blend in with the reddish-brown moss found in their natural habitat.

❧ ❧ ❧

Red pandas are excellent climbers and can descend trees headfirst.

❧ ❧ ❧

Their fur is waterproof, which helps keep them warm and dry in their damp habitats.

Red pandas are known to be very clean animals, often grooming themselves like cats.

∨ ∨ ∨

They use their bushy tails for balance while climbing and as a blanket to keep warm.

∨ ∨ ∨

Red pandas have fur on the soles of their feet to provide traction and insulation.

∨ ∨ ∨

Red pandas can close their nostrils to keep out debris while foraging for food.

Red pandas don't hibernate but will lower their metabolic rate during winter to save energy.

Red pandas have a
slow reproductive
rate, which contributes
to their vulnerable
conservation status.

They have a unique mating ritual that involves chasing, head bobbing, and vocalizations.

ಌ ಌ ಌ

Female red pandas build nests in hollow trees to give birth to their cubs.

ಌ ಌ ಌ

Red pandas have a life expectancy of around 8 to 10 years in the wild but can live up to 15 years in captivity.

ಌ ಌ ಌ

They are excellent swimmers, but generally avoid water.

Red pandas have been known to use their sharp claws to defend themselves against predators. Predators of the red panda include snow leopards, martens, and birds of prey.

❧ ❧ ❧

The red panda is the state animal of the Indian state of Sikkim.

❧ ❧ ❧

The name "panda" comes from the Nepali word "ponya," which means "bamboo eater."

❧ ❧ ❧

The red panda is considered a "living fossil" because of its unique evolutionary lineage.

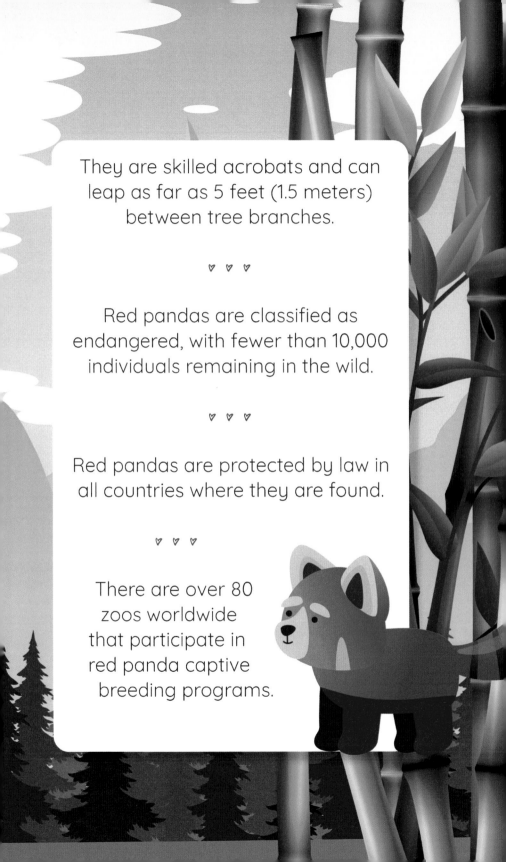

They are skilled acrobats and can leap as far as 5 feet (1.5 meters) between tree branches.

ᵥ ᵥ ᵥ

Red pandas are classified as endangered, with fewer than 10,000 individuals remaining in the wild.

ᵥ ᵥ ᵥ

Red pandas are protected by law in all countries where they are found.

ᵥ ᵥ ᵥ

There are over 80 zoos worldwide that participate in red panda captive breeding programs.

Did you know that the character Master Shifu from the popular animated movie "Kung Fu Panda" is inspired by a red panda?

The red panda's scientific name, Ailurus fulgens, means "shining cat" in Greek and Latin.

♥ ♥ ♥

International Red Panda Day is celebrated on the third Saturday of September every year to raise awareness about red panda conservation.

♥ ♥ ♥

Red pandas have a unique dental structure, with an extra molar on their lower jaw that helps them grind bamboo.

♥ ♥ ♥

Red pandas are known to wash their faces and body with their paws, similar to how raccoons do.

They have a highly sensitive sense of smell, which they use to locate food and detect predators.

❧ ❧ ❧

Red pandas have a slow metabolism to conserve energy, given their low-calorie bamboo diet.

❧ ❧ ❧

They are considered good luck symbols in some cultures and are thought to bring happiness and prosperity.

❧ ❧ ❧

The red panda was discovered by Western science in 1825, almost 50 years before the discovery of the giant panda.

Red pandas have a small, pink tongue covered in tiny hair-like structures called papillae.

Red Panda

QUIZ

Were you paying attention?! Test your new red panda knowledge in our quiz!

1   **What family do red pandas belong to?**

2   **What is the primary food source for red pandas?**

3   **Which two countries have the largest red panda populations?**

4   Where does the name "panda" come from?

5   What is a unique feature of red pandas' front paws that helps them grip bamboo?

6   What is the meaning of "crepuscular"?

7   What is the life expectancy of red pandas in the wild?

8   What is the scientific name for the red panda?

9   What kind of predators do red pandas have in the wild?

10 What are the two main threats to red pandas in the wild?

11 What is the term for red pandas' unique vocalization?

12 What do red pandas use their long, bushy tails for?

13 In which Indian state is the red panda the state animal?

14 What type of forests do red pandas primarily live in?

15 How do red pandas communicate with each other?

16 What unique ability do red pandas have in relation to tasting artificial sweeteners?

ANSWERS

1. Ailuridae
2. Bamboo
3. Nepal and China
4. It comes from the Nepali word "ponya," which means "bamboo eater."
5. A false thumb, which is an elongated wrist bone
6. Most active at dawn and dusk
7. Around 8 to 10 years
8. Ailurus fulgens
9. Snow leopards, martens, and birds of prey
10. Habitat loss and poaching
11. Twitter
12. For balance and warmth
13. Sikkim
14. Temperate forests

15. Through vocalizations, body language, and scent marking
16. They can taste artificial sweeteners, a rare ability among mammals
17. In hollow trees
18. About a year
19. Using scent glands in their feet
20. The Red Panda Dance

RED PANDAS

WORD SEARCH

```
H F D M A M M A L C X Z
T I C X H K G D S E F G
R A M B R E D P A N D A
F G F A S N C C V B G D
U F Q S L D C V U N H G
L I Y Q A A Z X C B B V
G R T W E N Y H G D S E
E E R Q V G B A M B O O
N F W Q C E Z C S B V X
S O D F O R E S T Q J G
G X F T D E C B J G D S
F S G C V D N B V X D F
```

Can you find all the words below in the word search puzzle on the left?

BAMBOO **ENDANGERED** **MAMMAL**

HIMALAYAS **RED PANDA** **FULGENS**

FIREFOX **CUBS** **FOREST**

SOLUTION

H			M	A	M	M	A	L			
	I										
		M		R	E	D	P	A	N	D	A
F		A		N		C					
U	F			L		D		U			
L	I			A				B			
G	R			N	Y				S		
E	E			G	B	A	M	B	O	O	O
N	F			E			S				
S	O		F	O	R	E	S	T			
	X			E							
				D							

SOURCES

Choudhury, A., 2001. An overview of the status and conservation of the red panda Ailurus fulgens in India, with reference to its global status. Oryx, 35(3), pp.250-259.

Glatston, A.R., 2011. Red Panda: Biology and Conservation of the First Panda. London: Academic Press.

Glatston, A.R., Wei, F., Zaw, T., and Sherpa, A., 2015. Ailurus fulgens. The IUCN Red List of Threatened Species 2015. Available at: https://www.iucnredlist.org/species/714/110023718 [Accessed 12 April 2023].

Pradhan, S., Saha, G.K., and Khan, J.A., 2001. Ecology of the red panda Ailurus fulgens in the Singhalila National Park, Darjeeling, India. Biological Conservation, 98(1), pp.11-18.

Red Panda Network, n.d. About Red Pandas. Available at: https://www.redpandanetwork.org/red_panda/about-red-panda/ [Accessed 12 April 2023].

Roberts, M.S. and Gittleman, J.L., 1984. Ailurus fulgens. Mammalian Species, 222, pp.1-8.

Wei, F., Feng, Z., Wang, Z. and Hu, J., 1999. Current distribution, status and conservation of wild red pandas Ailurus fulgens in China. Biological Conservation, 89(3), pp.285-291.

World Wildlife Fund, n.d. Red Panda. Available at: https://www.worldwildlife.org/species/red-panda [Accessed 12 April 2023].

Magazine, Smithsonian, and Corryn Wetzel. 2022. "Before Seeing 'Turning Red,' Learn These Amazing Red Panda Facts". Smithsonian Magazine. https://www.smithsonianmag.com/science-nature/eight-amazing-facts-about-red-pandas-180979708/.

"Fun Facts About Red Pandas • Red Panda Facts & Info For Kids". 2019. Folly Farm. https://www.folly-farm.co.uk/zoo/meet-the-zoo-animals/red-panda/.

"15 Fantastic Facts About Red Pandas". 2023. Redpandanetwork.Org. https://redpandanetwork.org/post/15-Fantastic-Facts-about-Red-Pandas.

"Top 5 Facts About Red Pandas". 2023. WWF. https://www.wwf.org.uk/learn/fascinating-facts/red-panda.

You're Red Pand-tastic!

As our delightful journey through the world of red pandas comes to an end, we hope you've enjoyed learning about these fascinating animals as much as we enjoyed sharing their story with you.

Your feedback means a lot to us, so we kindly ask you to leave a **review** on the platform where you purchased the book.

Your thoughts and experiences will help other readers discover the captivating world of red pandas and encourage us to continue creating engaging and educational content for all.

Thank you for your support, and may the spirit of these adorable creatures continue to inspire you!

ALSO BY JENNY KELLETT

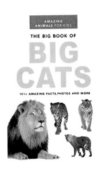

... and more!

Available at
www.bellanovabooks.com
and all major online bookstores.

·

Made in the USA
Las Vegas, NV
04 January 2024